Wanted!

Godly Women

By Linda Singletary

Linda Singletary's books are available at special quantity discounts to use as premiums and sales promotions, or for use in training programs. To place a bulk order, please contact Linda Singletary at linda@lindasingletary.com.

ISBN-13: 978-1514819678

ISBN-10: 1514819678

Printed in the United States of America

Dedication

I dedicate this series of lessons on "The Virtous Woman" to my husband, Bert, who for the past 43 years has helped me to become a godly woman. He has been more than a husband to me. He has been my pastor and has faithfully instructed me in God's Word. He has been my friend and has listened to me when I was down, and he has been my encourager in all my endeavours. For the past few months we have been traveling, and I was finding it difficult to prepare these lessons. I thank him for buying me a laptop computer, which made it possible to complete my preparations.

I love you, Bert, and appreciate all that you have done and still do for me.

Linda
2003

All scriptures in this book are taken from the King James Bible.

Other books by this author:

A Garden of Roses is Jesus

Being a Contented Christian

Being a Fruitful Christian

Being a Teachabe Christian

How About Your Heart?

It's a Jungle Out There

The Beauty of Holiness

Walk in the Spirit

Table of Contents

Lesson One

"She is Valuable"

"She is Valuable"

"…her price is far above rubies." Proverbs 31:10

As a young girl I loved to visit my grandparent's farm. I have fond memories of the time I spent there each summer. One of those memories is of a jewelry box on the dresser of the room where I often slept. In it was a ruby ring that had belonged to my mother. I don't know why she no longer wore the ring, other than that she did not wear much jewelry and she had replaced it with her wedding ring. I had been told that when the ring fit me it would be mine, and so each time I went to the farm I tried on the ring only to be disappointed that it was still too big. One day when I was about twelve years old, I was excited to discover that the ring fit and I was allowed to take it home with me. A few months later, as I was boarding the bus to go home from school, I noticed that the ruby was missing from my ring. I searched for it and was heartbroken when I never found it. As a result of this incident the ruby has been my favorite gem and on my fortieth wedding anniversary my husband surprised me with a ruby ring, pendant and earrings. Though he had never seen the original ring, the new ring was the same emerald cut as the one I had lost.

The Virtuous Woman is Valuable to God

The diamond may be considered "a girl's best friend" but the ruby is the rarest, and, in large sizes, the costliest of all the gems. In Prov. 31:10, the virtuous woman is compared to the ruby. Just as a ruby is rare, this verse indicates that a virtuous woman is also rare. "Who can find a virtuous woman?" In today's world, I believe we could even say she is indeed, very rare. If the ruby is costly the virtuous woman is even more costly for the verse says"…her price is far above rubies." Noah Webster's 1828 American Dictionary of the English Language defines virtuous as "morally good; acting in conformity to the moral law; practicing the moral duties, and abstaining from vice."

She is an example of what God intended a woman to be. The New Testament speaks of how God knows even when a sparrow falls to the ground and we read in Matt. 10:31, "Fear ye not therefore, ye are of more value than many sparrows." All of mankind is valuable to God but the virtuous woman is of even more value -- "her price is far above rubies."

The Virtuous Woman is Valuable to Her Husband

He values her companionship:

In the Garden of Eden, though Adam was surrounded by animals, God saw that he was still lonely--there was no one just like him. Woman was created for the special purpose of fulfilling Adam's need for companionship. Gen. 2:18, "And the LORD God said, It is not good that a man should be alone; I will make him an help meet for him." Though God made woman to help man, He did not make her of any less value or any less importance. A man is usually physically stronger than a woman but God made him to be dependent upon her for many things. My husband can look right at something and never see it, so he calls me to show him where it is. He needs me to match his socks and iron his shirts, but most of all he needs me to be his friend, confident and companion. God made woman as a special gift for man. He made her to be man's completer and in I Cor. 11:7-9 we read, "the woman is the glory of the man. For man is not of the woman; but woman of the man. Neither was the man created for the woman; but the woman for the man."

In this day of women's rights we are often told that we should fight to be equal with men, and we are made to feel that not to do the same things that a man does is to be inferior to him. Of course, this is not true. In our home my husband and I have different roles. I am happy to let my husband change flat tires and crawl under the car when something is wrong. I like it that he shovels snow and repairs leaky faucets. I have no desire to do his jobs. He, in turn, enjoys the special meals that I prepare for him and having clean clothes ready to wear. Though we have different roles, we are both valuable to God, and to each other.

Gen. 2:21-24, "And the LORD God caused a deep sleep to fall upon Adam, and he slept: and he took one of his ribs, and closed up the flesh instead thereof; and the rib, which the LORD God had taken from man, made he a woman, and brought her unto the man. And Adam said, This is now bone of my bones, and flesh of my flesh: she shall be called Woman, because she was taken out of Man. Therefore, shall a man leave his father and his mother, and shall cleave unto his wife: and they shall be one flesh." The ribs are found near the heart. God made the woman from the rib of the man that she might be cherished and held near his heart. God made them to be one flesh and He intended that a man should treat his wife as he would his own flesh. Eph. 5:29, "For no man ever yet hated his own flesh; but nourisheth and cherisheth it, even as the Lord the church." God instructed men in Eph. 5:25, "Husbands, love your wives, even as Christ also loved the church, and gave himself for it." A husband should have the same unconditional love for his wife as Christ had for the church. God made him to be her protector and he should be willing to give his life for her.

He values her submission:

The wife, in turn, should choose to submit to her husband. Eph. 5:22-24, "Wives, submit yourselves to your own husbands, as unto the Lord. For the husband is the head of the wife, even as Christ is the head of the church: and he is the saviour of the body. Therefore as the church is subject unto Christ, so let the wives be to their own husbands in every thing." As women, we do not like the word "submission" but we must realize that submission has nothing to do with value, intelligence, talent or ability, but rather with order. God is a God of order and He made all of His creation in an orderly way. For anything to operate properly there must be a head or an authority, and God made the man to be the head of the home. I Cor. 11:3, "But I would have you know, that the head of every man is Christ; and the head of every woman is the man; and the head of Christ is God."

When Adam followed Eve and ate of the forbidden fruit in the Garden of Eden he gave his headship to Eve and she turned her headship over to Satan, the prince of the power of the air, who is now trying to run the world. As a result of Eve's sin God told her in Gen. 3:16, "...and thy desire shall be to thy husband, and he shall rule over thee." At that same time man received his own curse for Adam's sin of hearkening to his wife. He would have to fight the thorns and thistles as he tilled the land to provide for his wife and family. When a woman submits to her husband she is submitting to the Lord. It is impossible to be submissive to the Lord without being submissive to your husband.

Notice that the Bible does not instruct the woman to be in submission to men in general, but to be in submission to her own husband. In Col. 3:18 God instructs "Wives, submit yourselves unto your own husbands" but He goes on to say in Col.

3:19 "Husbands, love your wives, and be not bitter against them." Submission is a response to love and love a response to submission. Though there is no command in the Bible for wives to love their husbands, in Tit. 2:4 the aged women are told to teach the young women to "love their husbands." Another interesting fact is that both husband and wife are told to submit to each other. Eph. 5:21, "Submitting yourselves one to another in the fear of God." Phil. 2:3, speaks to people in general by saying, "...in lowliness of mind let each esteem other better than themselves." It is especially important in a marriage for both husband and wife to follow this principle. When a husband and wife are both obedient to God in love and submission they will have a successful marriage.

When a woman is married to a man who is not saved and not obedient to the Lord, is she still supposed to submit to him? I Pet. 3:1, "Likewise, ye wives, be in subjection to your own husbands; that, if any obey not the word, they also may without the word be won by the conversation of the wives." A woman should be submissive to her husband as long as he does not lead her contrary to God's Word, and this submission may bring her husband to salvation. Submission encourages love and love encourages submission. Your husband will value your submission just as you value his love.

He values her ideas:
The Bible speaks of Sarah as being a submissive and obedient woman. I Pet. 3:6, "Even as Sara obeyed Abraham, calling him lord." This does not mean that Sarah worshipped Abraham but rather that she reverenced and respected him. When we read about their lives in the book of Genesis we find that Abraham made a positive response to her submission by listening to her ideas. Even though her ideas were not always good he seemed to do everything that she suggested. It was her idea for Abram to bear a son by her handmaid Hagar. Gen. 16:2, "And Sarai said unto Abram, Behold now, the LORD hath restrained me from bearing: I pray thee, go in unto my maid; it may be that I may obtain children by her. And Abram hearkened to the voice of Sarai." Later, even though it grieved him, Abraham listened to her when she asked him to cast out Hagar and her son. Gen. 21:10, "Wherefore she said unto Abraham, Cast out this bondwoman and her son: for the son of this bondwoman shall not be heir with my son, even with Isaac." Because we have the instructions in God's Word, which Sarah did not have, hopefully we will have better advice to offer our husbands today.

In a Christ honoring home a husband and wife should discuss and pray about decisions that need to be made. The husband should listen to the wife's ideas, but after seeking God's leading he should make the final decisions. The woman should accept his choices knowing that he is responsible to God for his decisions.

Prov. 12:4, "A virtuous woman is a crown to her husband:" Strive to live a virtuous life and be a shinning crown so that your husband will be proud to call you his wife. The more honor and respect you show to him the more honor and respect you will receive in return. Remember, a virtuous woman is more valuable than rubies.

Questions:

1. What jewel is the virtuous woman compared to in Prov. 31:10?

    _____

2. According to Gen. 2:18 God made woman to be an

    _____ for man.

3. God says in Gen. 2:24 that a husband and wife should be one

    _____.

4. According to Eph. 5:25 how is a husband to love his wife?

    _____

5. What advise does God give to the wife in Eph. 5:22?

    _____

6. Can a woman be in submission to the Lord without being in submission
    to her husband? _____

7. What might be the results of a woman's submission to an unsaved
    husband? I Pet. 3:1 _____

8. What Bible woman called her husband lord? I Pet. 3:6 _____

9. According to Prov. 12:4 a virtuous woman is a _____
    to her husband.

Lesson Two

"She is Trustworthy"

"She is Trustworthy"

"...her husband doth safely trust in her." Proverbs 31:11

In Bible days when armies went to war they often returned with the "spoil" or plunder taken from the enemy in the captured city. This spoil could consist of anything considered valuable including animals and even women and children. Deut. 20:14, "But the women, and the little ones, and the cattle, and all that is in the city, even all the spoil thereof, thou shalt take unto thyself; and thou shalt eat of the spoil of thine enemies, which the LORD thy God hath given thee." As in this verse, the army was sometimes given permission to keep the spoil and at other times it was not. The virtuous woman in Prov. 31:11 was trusted by her husband and was such a help to him that he had no reason to keep the spoil. "The heart of her husband doth safely trust in her, so that he shall have no need of spoil." Today's godly woman should be just as trustworthy to her husband.

The Virtuous Woman can be Trusted with the Finances

The husband and wife should be a team and should be in agreement as to how the home is run and the money is spent. Together they should set up a budget and should try to live within their means no matter whether the income is large or small. We live in a day of affluence when people think they must have the newest and best of everything. This idea is fine for those with a big paycheck, but for those on a limited income it can lead to serious problems.

As a "keeper of the home" (Tit. 2:5) the wife is responsible for much of the spending and she should learn to stretch her dollars by becoming a wise shopper. It may be challenging to feed a family tasty, well-balanced meals on a limited budget, but it can be done and can be very rewarding. How satisfying it can be to turn sale items and an inexpensive cut of meat into a delicious meal. It may be difficult to clothe a family and decorate a home with yard sale and thrift store finds, but doing so affords an opportunity to be creative and produces a real sense of accomplishment.

When living on a limited income even the little things count. Remember that pennies add up to dollars. Several years ago my teenage daughter and her friend were watching me cook. My daughter was embarrassed when I washed a piece a aluminum foil so that it could be reused. She did not want her friend to think that I was such a cheapskate, but being raised in a pastor's home my mother had taught me to be frugal.   A couple of years ago her friend, who is now the mother of five children including two sets of twins, emailed me to say that she still remembered that day and now often does the same thing.

A friend told me a similar story of how her granddaughter made fun of her for recycling aluminum foil, but that same granddaughter had declared bankruptcy because she was unable to pay her bills.   Because I have been careful in spending money we have been able to enjoy things we could not otherwise have afforded. While I am not saying that recycling aluminum foil and shopping yard sales are necessary for becoming a godly woman, a godly woman will do everything that it takes to live within her budget.

We live in a day when people declare bankruptcy at the drop of a hat. Unwise use of credit cards is often responsible for bankruptcy. Credit is so easy to obtain and so hard to control. Be careful about buying things that you cannot afford. Paying high rates of interest each month is like pouring water down the drain and robs you of both money and peace of mind. It is much more enjoyable to save up for a purchase and pay cash than it is to worry about how you are going to pay the bills at the end of the month, or worse yet, to still be paying for something long after it is worn out.   Declaring bankruptcy may legally rid you from your debts but it does not morally free you from those obligations.

The Shopper's Prayer

Lord,
When the stores cry out my name,
Help me not to play their game.
Remind me what I have at home--
The bargains I already own.
When "Open!" "Open!" fills my ears,
Replace them with my checkbook fears.
Protect me, Lord, from senseless greed,
For simple things are all I need.
Rebecca Barlow Jordan

The Virtuous Woman can be Trusted with the Children

God's plan is for the husband to be the head of the home and to provide for his family's physical and spiritual needs. Many men, however, fail in the responsibility concerning raising the children and think that this is the woman's job. They need to become familiar with Eph. 6:4, "And, ye fathers, provoke not your children to wrath: but bring them up in the nurture and admonition of the Lord." We might say that the husband is the head of the home and the wife is the heart of the home.

Since the wife does normally spend more time with the children, the husband should be able to trust her to assist him with this nurturing and admonishing of the children. They should share the same goals and desires for their family and should never undermine one another in the disciplining of the children. Both husband and wife should work together to accomplish the admonition given in Deut. 6:6-7, "And these words, which I command thee this day, shall be in thine heart: And thou shalt teach them diligently unto thy children, and shalt talk of them when thou sittest in thine house, and when thou walkest by the way, and when thou liest down, and when thou risest up."

The husband should also be able to trust the wife to set a good example for the children in both her behavior and her dress. We are often appalled by the way teenage girls dress today, but many times they are following in their mother's footsteps. A friend of mine had a teenage daughter who attended public school. One day she commented to her mother about how girls must change their clothes after they left home and before they arrive at school, because she did not believe their mothers would let them come dressed as they did. How sad that more mothers were not like her mother. Many mothers not only allow their daughters to dress immodestly but dress that way themselves.

The Virtuous Woman can be Trusted to do Good

Prov. 31:12, "She will do him good and not evil all the days of her life." Prov. 18:22, "Whoso findeth a wife findeth a good thing, and obtained favour of the LORD." A good wife will lift up her husband by encouraging him when he is down.

She will not criticize him in front of the children or other people, but will speak privately with him about any differences they might have.

The Virtuous Woman can be Trusted to be Faithful

Prov. 12:4b, "...but she that maketh ashamed is as rottenness in his bones." A godly woman will take her wedding vows very seriously. "For better or for worse" means just that. She will faithfully stand by her husband in the bad times just as she does in the good times. She will have eyes for him only. She will meet her husband's needs "so that he shall have no need of spoil." When a wife is faithful to the Lord, she will have no problem being faithful to her husband. Love is the glue that holds a marriage together. No husband or wife is perfect but when a marriage is filled with love, faults are more easily overlooked. I Pet. 4:8, "And above all things have fervent charity (love) among yourselves: for charity shall cover the multitude of sins." If you are having trouble with your love life think about how God loved an undeserving sinner like yourself, and spend time reading and studying the book of I John.

I John 4:7-11, "Beloved, let us love one another: for love is of God; and every one that loveth is born of God, and knoweth God. He that loveth not knoweth not God; for God is love. In this was manifest the love of God toward us, because that God sent his only begotten Son into the world, that we might live through him. Herein is love, not that we loved God, but that he loved us, and sent his Son to be the propitiation for our sins. Beloved, if God so loved us, we ought also to love one another."

Are you a trustworthy wife?

Questions:

1. The virtuous woman could be safely _____
   by her husband. Prov. 31:11

2. In Prov. 31:11, what is meant by the word "spoil"? _____
   _____

3. What responsibility does God give to fathers in Eph. 6:4?
   _____

4. What admonition is given to parents in Deut. 6:6-7?
   _____
   _____

5. What is the "good thing" found in Prov. 18:22? _____

6. Prov. 12:4 says that to make your husband ashamed is as
   "_____."

7. I John 4:8 tells us that if we do not love we do not _____.

Lesson Three

"She is Industrious"

"She is Industrious"

"...worketh willing with her hands." Proverbs 31:13

This virtuous woman of Proverbs 31 is certainly a woman with great energy and could even be considered a "superwoman." We may never be able to keep up with her and do all the things that she did but God has given her as a pattern for us to follow. Methods have changed and we have many conveniences that she knew nothing about, but the principles remain the same and we can learn much from her example.

The Virtuous Woman is a Willing Worker

There is an old saying which is certainly true -- "a man works from sun to sun but a woman's work is never done." As a "keeper of the home" there is no end to all the jobs that are required of a woman each day. When a woman marries she is accepting some big responsibilities. She should consider this before she says "I do." If she is not ready for these tasks she might want to reconsider her decision to marry or maybe look for a millionaire who could provide her with maid service. She should not have to be begged or coerced into doing the expected tasks of running a home. I believe that God intended for couples to have children, but bringing children into the home brings many more responsibilities as well as many blessings.

Not only should she be a willing worker, but she should also be willing to rise early or stay up late if that is what is necessary to meet her family's needs. Prov. 31:15, "She riseth also while it is yet night," and Prov. 31:18, "her candle goeth not out by night." Many times a mother is called upon to get up in the middle of the night to tend a sick child. Those memories were recently refreshed in my mind when I kept my two granddaughters for a week. Amidst all the fun we had that week there was one night that was not so much fun. That night I was up and down with a sick little girl. It was her mother that she really wanted but since Momma was 600 miles away she settled for Nana, and I willingly tended to her needs. How glad I was that she was feeling better the next day because I was ready to get some sleep.

The Virtuous Woman is not Lazy

Prov. 31:27, "She looketh well to the ways of her household, and eateth not the bread of idleness." With all the things that the Proverbs 31 lady did, I don't believe that she would have had much time to watch the "soaps" or gossip on the phone even if she would have had a television and a telephone. Neither should today's godly woman allow her precious time to be spent so foolishly. It is wonderful to have access to a telephone but be careful not to let the phone occupy your day.

An occasional TV program can be relaxing but most programs are not worth watching and can be damaging for children to watch. Screen what comes into your home and be sure you don't overdose on TV. A good rule to follow is not to turn on the television until you have spent some time with the Lord and finished your housework. As for your children, their homework should always take priority over TV. Many children have become couch potatoes as they sit for hours in front of the TV. To develop strong bodies children need outdoor activities. To develop strong minds they need to be read stories and they need time for creative play.

The lazy woman is shortchanging herself. She is depriving herself of things that are obtained by hard work. Prov. 13:4, "The soul of the sluggard desireth, and hath nothing: but the soul of the diligent shall be made fat." Prov. 20:4, "The sluggard will not plow by reason of the cold; therefore shall he beg in harvest, and have nothing."

The Virtuous Woman Meets her Family's Needs

She feeds her family well:

Prov. 31:15, "…and giveth meat to her household." The Proverbs 31 lady had a garden to help provide food for her family. Prov. 31:16, "…with the fruit of her hands she planted a vineyard." You may have to settle for a tomato plant in the flowerbed or maybe no garden at all, but you should do your best to provide good, nourishing meals for your family and still stay within your budget. The virtuous woman appears to have been quite a shopper because Prov. 31:14 says "She is like the merchants' ships; she bringeth her food from afar." This indicates that convenience was not her main concern. She did not do all her shopping at the Circle K, but was willing to look around for the best bargains. I don't believe a daily diet of fast food fare would have been acceptable to the virtuous woman of Proverbs 31, nor is it very healthy for families today.

She clothes her family well:

Not only was the Proverbs 31 woman an accomplished seamstress, she also spun the thread and wove the cloth. Prov. 31:13, "She seeketh wool and flax." Prov. 31:19, "She layeth her hands to the spindle, and her hands hold the distaff." The clothing she made for herself was the very best. Prov. 31:22, "She maketh herself coverings of tapestry; her clothing is silk and purple." Her husband never had to hang his head because of the way he was clothed.

Prov. 31:23, "Her husband is known in the gates, when he sitteth among the elders of the land." Her wise shopping no doubt contributed to her ability to dress her family so luxuriously. You may not have the resources to clothe your family as well as she did, but do the best with what you have and remember how important cleanliness is. A little soap and water go a long way in making someone look and smell good. Ironing really improves the looks of a garment.

I praise the Lord that the methods for clothing a family are easier today than they were in the days of Proverbs 31. I often sewed when I was raising my family but I never had to make the material or seek the wool and flax. I do very little sewing today because I have discovered that if I can wait until the end of the season stores offer wonderful sales. Children's clothes, sometimes like new, can often be purchased for pennies at thrift stores and yard sales. Whether you sew or buy your families' clothes ready made, the object is to dress them as well as possible without spending more than your budget allows.

The Virtuous Woman Contributes to the Family Income

The virtuous woman of Proverbs 31 not only clothed her family but she supplemented their income by making and selling things to others. Prov. 31:24, "She maketh fine linen and selleth it; and delivered girdles unto the merchant." The average woman in today's society works at a job outside of the home. Many women choose to have a career and spend years training for that career and feel that they must use their training. Others believe their family could not make it without that second income. Whether to work or not to work is a decision you and your husband should pray about and decide upon together, preferably before you get married. No matter what decision you make you must always remember that your family should have priority over your job. Juggling a family and a job is quite an undertaking and homes are suffering today because women don't have time for their husband and children.

Working from the home might be a good alternative for women who need to supplement the family income. Some women choose to care for other children so that they can stay home with their own. Another option is to work during the hours that your children are in school. Whether a woman is a working mother or a stay-at-home mom, children need to be taught to share in the housework. This helps out the mother and is good training for the children.

I thank the Lord that I never had to work a job outside of our home. Of course, being a pastor's wife and working around the church was often equal to a job--minus the paycheck. I felt that I contributed to our family income by being extra careful with how I spent money. Ask the Lord to guide you in what would be best for you and your family. Make sure that in all your duties you still have time to honor the Lord.

Being a wife and mother can be overwhelming in today's busy world. Make sure that in all your duties you make time to spend with the Lord by reading His Word, praying and attending church regularly. No matter how talented you are or how much energy you have you will do a better job when you seek His leading on a daily basis. On days when you think you just can't make it turn to Him. Phil. 4:13, "I can do all things through Christ which strengtheneth me."

Questions:

1. In Prov. 31:13 we find that the virtuous woman was a _____ worker.

2. Prov. 31:15, 18 tell us that a lot of her work had to be done at

   _____.

3. How do we know that the virtuous woman was not lazy? Prov. 31:27

   _____

4. According to Prov. 20:4, what will the lazy woman have to do when it is time for the harvest? _____

5. In feeding her family she often brought her food from _____. Prov. 31:14

6. What materials did the virtuous woman seek in Prov. 31:13?

   _____

7. Prov. 31:22 tells us that her clothing was made of _____

   _____.

8. How did she contribute to her family income? Prov. 31:24 _____

   _____

9. What New Testament verse gives us hope that we can be an industrious, virtuous woman? _____

Lesson Four

"She is Prepared"

"She is Prepared"

"Prepare thy work." Psalm 24:27

In these busy days in which we live people often think they do not have time to prepare. Instead they just let things happen as they will. This lifestyle can contribute to many problems and in the long run actually wastes a lot of time. The Proverbs 31 woman made preparations and the godly woman today will do the same.

The Virtuous Woman Prepares for the Future

Prov. 31:21, "She is not afraid of the snow for her household: for all her household are clothed with scarlet." Many people live as if there were no tomorrow but the Proverbs 31 woman knew that winter would come and she prepared for it by making warm clothes for the family to wear. I am not sure of the significance of the word "scarlet," but scarlet was an expensive dye and this must mean that she prepared the very best clothing for her family. We might compare this to the beginning of a new school year when the kids will need new clothes, shoes and school supplies. This can be a difficult time financially but the wise woman will not wait until the day before school starts to get her children ready for school. She will set aside money throughout the year to prepare for these extra expenses.

The Bible speaks of the ant as being wise and in Prov. 30:25 says, "The ants are a people not strong, yet they prepare their meat in the summer." If the ants can make preparation surely we can do the same. Like the Proverbs 31 woman, my mother always grew a big garden and much of the summer was spent canning and freezing the harvest so that we would be prepared to eat during the winter. If it would not have been for the garden we would often have gone hungry. Since New Mexico is not a "garden state" we have not found a big garden to be very profitable, but I try to keep my pantry stocked so that I am prepared for unexpected company and whatever else might arise.

Husbands and wives should work together to be financially prepared for the future. Young couples should prepare to buy a home. Preparations need to be made to help the kids go to college, and it is wise to have insurance policies to prepare for illnesses and deaths. Don't just live for today. Make preparations for the future.

The Virtuous Woman Prepares for Eternity

More important than all the physical preparations that a woman might make is the spiritual preparation that she makes. Amos 4:12, "...prepare to meet thy God." A virtuous woman is a woman who has already made preparation to meet God by placing her trust in Jesus Christ. John 14:6, "Jesus saith unto him, I am the way, the truth, and the life: no man cometh unto the Father, but by me." Though she may be a very good person, she is not trusting in her good works, her baptism or her church membership; but in Christ and Christ alone for her salvation. If Christ were to return today she would be ready. Lk. 12:40, "Be ye therefore ready also, for the Son of man cometh at an hour when ye think not."

The Virtuous Woman Prepares for the Day

Women are so busy today and often have more on their daily schedule than can possibly be accomplished. Because of this we sometimes fail to prepare for the day. Most days we make some physical preparations. We get dressed (hopefully before noon), drink our coffee, and maybe even eat breakfast, but are we prepared for the fiery darts that Satan will hurl at us? We sometimes wonder why everything is going wrong. Could it be because we have neglected the most important thing of all--our quiet time with the Lord? We argue that we just don't have time to read our Bible and pray, but the truth is we don't have time not to do those things. We will find that things go so much smoother when we have taken time to spend with the Lord. Samuel told the Israelites in I Sam. 7:3 that if they wanted to be delivered from their enemies they needed to "put away the strange gods....and prepare your hearts unto the LORD." In the same way we need to confess and forsake our sins and prepare our hearts so that we will be ready for the trials that are sure to come our way.

The Virtuous Woman Prepares to be a Witness

Many women fail to witness for the Lord because they don't know what to say -- they are unprepared. The Apostle Peter wrote to the early Christians in I Pet 3:15, "But sanctify the Lord God in your hearts: and be ready always to give an answer to every man that asketh you a reason of the hope that is in you with meekness and fear." We cannot use our ignorance as an excuse for not being a witness. Instead, we should study God's Word and arm ourselves as we are told to do in Eph. 6:15, "And your feet shod with the preparation of the gospel of peace."

The Virtuous Woman Prepares for Sunday

Through my years as a pastor's wife I have noticed that people often did not come to church on Sunday morning because they were unprepared. They stayed up late on Saturday night, got up late Sunday morning and then found out there were no clean clothes hanging in the closet. A godly woman will not allow this to happen. She will think ahead and make sure the clothes are clean so that this excuse cannot keep her family away from church. A godly woman will not stay in the bed until the last minute on Sunday morning but will consider the amount of time needed to get ready for church. Allowing enough time to get ready can prevent arguments and confusion in the home.

Another preparation that needs to be made on Sunday morning is that of the heart. We should go to church for the purpose of worshipping the Lord and being fed from His Word, but many times our minds are so full of worry and care that we don't hear a word the pastor says.

A few months ago I was especially concerned about the care of my mother. As I left the church on Sunday morning I was convicted about how little I had gotten from the pastor's message, and knew that my worries had kept me from worshipping the Lord as I should have. That week I had been cleaning out a closet and had gotten rid of a lot of things. They were not bad things, but rather things that I no longer needed and that were just taking up space in my closet. The next morning in my devotions, the Lord spoke to me from Gen. 35:2-3, "Then Jacob said unto his household, and to all that were with him, Put away the strange gods that are among you, and be clean, and change your garments: And then arise, and go up to Bethel; and I will make there an altar unto God." Before Jacob took his family to Bethel, the house of God, he told them to get rid of their strange gods, to cleanse themselves and put on clean clothes. They needed to do some housecleaning to prepare for worship. I realized that worry was like a strange god and just as I had emptied my closet of junk, I needed to empty my mind of worry and concern and prepare my heart to worship before going to God's House.

My concerns were not bad things but they hindered my worship. We need to be like Ezra and prepare our hearts to seek the Lord. Ezra 7:10, "For Ezra had prepared his heart to seek the law of the LORD, and to do it." We will find our time at church to be much more meaningful when we have prepared our hearts to seek the Lord.

When we ask for God's help in preparing our hearts we can be assured He will hear us and answer our prayer. Ps. 10:17, "LORD, thou hast heard the desire of the humble: thou wilt prepare their heart, thou wilt cause thine ear to hear."

Questions:

1. How did the Proverbs 31 woman prepare for winter? Prov. 31:21
    _____

2. What insect does the Bible call wise because it prepared its meat in the summer? Prov. 30:25 _____

3. Amos 4:12 tells us to _____.

4. What is the reason given in Lk.12:40 for being ready?
    _____

5. What must we do to be really prepared for the day? _____

6. When should we be ready to give an answer concerning our hope in Christ? I Pet. 3:15_____

7. Our feet should be prepared to take the _____
    Eph. 6:15

8. Ezra 7:10, "For Ezra had _____ his heart to seek the law of the Lord"

Lesson Five

"She is Strong"

"She is Strong"

"Strength and honour are her clothing." Proverbs 31:25

The Virtuous Woman Needs Physical Strength

One would have to be physically strong to accomplish all that the Proverbs 31 lady accomplished. Prov. 31:17, "She girdeth her loins with strength." In Bible days a girdle was not an under-garment worn by a woman to conceal fat but rather a sash or belt worn around the loins for the purpose of support. The loin is the part of the body on each side of the spinal column and between the hip and the lower ribs. In many work places today employees are required to wear braces to prevent back strain when lifting heavy objects. This lady evidently took precautions to strengthen herself and to make herself safe when she worked.

Prov. 31:17, "...and strengthenth her arms." I doubt that this lady lifted weights but she evidently made an effort to increase her strength. She had a lot to do and a weak person can get very little work done. Today's godly woman also needs to take care of herself physically and build up her strength. She needs to eat right and get proper rest and exercise if she is to reach her full potential. To be unfit physically can limit our spiritual as well as our physical accomplishments.

The Virtuous Woman Needs Spiritual Strength

In chapter two we discussed how the Proverbs 31 woman spun thread, wove fabric and sewed beautiful, warm clothing for herself and her family and even sold her products to other people. It seemed that outward apparel was very important to this lady, but also important to her was her inner dress. Prov. 31:25, "Strength and honour are her clothing." I Pet. 3:3-4 stresses the importance of the inward clothing by saying, "Whose adorning let it not be that outward adorning of plaiting the hair, and of wearing gold, or of putting on of apparel: But let it be the hidden man of the heart, in that which is not corruptible, even the ornament of a meek and quiet spirit, which is in the sight of God of great price." I do not believe these verses are saying that we should not braid our hair or wear jewelry, but rather that we should not put more emphasis on our outward appearance than we do on our inward appearance. We should not take care of our physical needs at the expense of our spiritual needs. How can we clothe ourselves in strength?

The armor of the Lord gives strength:

Isa. 51:9, tells us to "Awake, awake, put on strength." It takes a conscientious effort to put on strength and become spiritually strong. Eph. 6:10-11 tell us to "be strong in the Lord" by putting on "the whole armour of God." Eph. 6:12-17 goes on to list the items of armor which are the girdle of truth, the breastplate of righteousness, the shoes of peace, the shield of faith, the helmet of salvation and the sword of the Spirit. When we arise each morning we need to ask the Lord to clothe us in His armor so that we can stand strong against the trials that may come our way that day.

The way of the Lord gives strength:

Prov. 10:29, "The way of the Lord is strength to the upright." Ps. 18:32, "It is God that girdeth me with strength, and maketh my way perfect." When we walk in God's way and obey His word He will gird us with His strength.

The wisdom of the Lord gives strength:

Ecc. 7:18-19, "…for he that feareth God shall come forth of them all. Wisdom strengthened the wise more than ten mighty men which are in the city." Prov. 9:10, "The fear of the LORD is the beginning of wisdom:" These verses tell us that wisdom helps us to develop strength and that in order to be truly wise we must fear the Lord. To fear the Lord is to reverence and trust the Lord so much that we would be afraid not to obey Him. To obey the Lord reveals both wisdom and strength.

The joy of the Lord gives strength:

Neh. 8:10, "…for the joy of the LORD is your strength." Troubles can weigh us down and zap our strength but when we concentrate on our blessings and rejoice at what the Lord has done for us we soon forget about our troubles, which are usually very small in comparison to our many blessing. On several occasions when I have been extremely tired I have found renewed strength by simply spending some time counting my blessings and praising the Lord. Ps. 71:14-16, "But I will hope continually, and will yet praise thee more and more. My mouth shall shew forth thy righteousness and thy salvation all the day; for I know not the numbers thereof. I will go in the strength of the Lord GOD; I will make mention of thy righteousness, even of thine only."

To wait on the Lord gives strength:

One of my favorite verses is Isa. 40:31, "But they that wait upon the LORD shall renew their strength; they shall mount up with wings as eagles; they shall run, and not be weary; and they shall walk, and not faint." It is not easy to wait but we receive strength as we wait on the Lord. Our pace of life is so fast these days that we often think we do not have time to wait on the Lord. We rush ahead of the Lord and do things in the flesh and then wonder how we got into such a mess. To wait on the Lord does not mean to sit around doing nothing, but rather to seek His leading about everything we do. Just as a waiter in a restaurant stands by the table ready to take your order and serve you, we should be ready to follow God's orders and serve Him. A good waiter or waitress would never serve our food before finding out what we wanted, but we often try to serve God without considering what He wants us to do.

We must be dependent upon the Lord for strength:

When we are at our weakest point we can best experience God's strength because it is in our time of need that we must rely on Him. II Cor. 12:9, "And he said unto me, My grace is sufficient for thee: for my strength is made perfect in weakness." When God chose Gideon to deliver the Israelites from the hand of the Midianites, Gideon realized his weakness and said in Jud. 6:15, "Oh my Lord, wherewith shall I save Israel? Behold, my family is poor in Manasseh, and I am the least in my father's house." The Lord promised to be with Gideon and give the Israelites victory even though they were out-numbered by the Midianites. Just to make sure that the Israelites would not fight this battle in their own strength, God lead Gideon to reduce his army of 32,000 men down to a mere 300 men. They had no choice but to go in the strength of the Lord. When the Israelites won the battle there was no doubt that God alone had given them the victory.

We can be assured that if God asks us to do a job and if we wait upon Him that no matter how weak and helpless we may be He will provide the strength to accomplish the task. Phil. 4:13, "I can do all things through Christ which strengthened me." Many times God waits until the moment of need to dispense this strength. My verse for this year, 2003, has been Deut. 33:25, "…as thy days, so shall thy strength be." Many days when I have been tired and felt that I just could not do all that needed to be done, the Lord has given me just the amount of strength I needed to make it through the day. In His grace He has been my sufficiency. Praise His name!

Questions:

1. With what did the virtuous woman gird her loins? _____

2. Prov. 31:25 says that "_____ and _____ were her clothing."

3. I Pet. 3:4 tells us that a _____ is in the sight of God of great price.

4. We can become strong by putting on the _____. Eph. 6:10-11

5. "Wisdom strengthened the wise more than _____. Ecc. 7:19

6. "The _____ is your strength." Neh. 8:12

7. A good way to renew our strength is by _____ Isa. 40:31

8. II Cor. 12:9 tells us that God's strength is made perfect in our

   _____.

9. In Jud. 6 who depended upon the Lord for strength to win a battle?

   _____

10. God's promise in Deut. 33:25 says "as thy days, so shall thy

    _____ be.

Lesson Six

"She is Benevolent"

"She is Benevolent"

"She stretcheth out her hand to the poor; yea, she reacheth forth her hands to the needy." Proverbs 31:20

Not only did this Proverbs 31 woman work hard and take good care of her family, she also cared about and shared with others. Prov. 31:20, "She stretcheth out her hand to the poor; yea, she reacheth forth her hands to the needy." This stretching and reaching out to the poor and needy could have included many things such as being a friend in time of need, opening her home for entertaining, sharing her possessions with those less fortunate, and giving of her talents and her time to assist others. When we give ourselves and everything we have to the Lord we have no trouble giving to others. Rom. 12:1, "I beseech you therefore, brethren, by the mercies of God, that ye present your bodies a living sacrifice, holy, acceptable unto God, which is your reasonable service."

The Virtuous Woman Gives of Her Possessions to the Lord

When we give to God, He promises to meet our needs and I have seen that happen over and over in my life. The Apostle Paul thanked the church in Philippi because they gave to him. Because they gave, he told them in Phil. 4:19, "But my God shall supply all your need according to his riches in glory by Christ Jesus." One does not need to be rich in order to give. Through the years I have noticed it was often thoes that had the least that gave the most, and they seemed to find joy in therir giving.

The Macedonian church joyfully gave out of their poverty. II Cor. 8:2, "How that in a great trial of affliction the abundance of their joy and their deep poverty abounded unto the riches of their liberality." Because they had first given themselves to the Lord they were able to give their possessions to the Lord. II Cor 8:5, "...but first gave their own selves to the Lord, and unto us by the will of God."

We just can't outgive God. When we give to Him by giving to others He seems to give us more in return. He may not give us wealth, but He certainly does give us blessing. Prov. 11:25, "The liberal soul shall be made fat: and he that watereth shall be watered also himself."

I John 3: 17-18 has some harsh words about our unwillingness to give. "But whoso hath this world's good, and seeth his brother have need, and shutteth up his bowels of compasion from him, how dwelleth the love of God in him? My little children, let us not love in word, neither in tongue; but in deed and in truth."

The Virtuous Woman Gives of Her Talents to the Lord

The Proverbs 31 woman seemed to have special talents in sewing and gardening and probably used them to minister to the poor and needy. We all have different talents and we should be willing to use whatever we have to help others. Dorcas was a New Testament lady who used her time and talents to help others. Acts 9:36, "Now there was at Joppa a certain disciple named Tabitha, which by interpretation is called Dorcas: this woman was full of good works and alms deeds which she did." Acts 9:39 goes on to tells us that Dorcas helped the widows by making them coats and garments. When Dorcas died all of these widows whom she had sewed for gathered around and wept. How were they going to survive without the help of Dorcas? Seeing their distress the disciples in Joppa sent for Peter who then prayed and called Dorcas back to life. As a result of this miracle many people throughout Joppa came to know the Lord. Giving can be a means of showing others the love of Christ, which in turn may give us an opportunity to lead them to know the Lord.

The Virtuous Woman Gives Her Home to the Lord

Just as our possessions, our time, and our talents should be given to the Lord, so should our home belong to Him. II Kings 4:8-11 tells the story of the great woman of Shunem who fed the prophet Elisha each time he passed by. Later she prevailed upon her husband to build a little chamber on the wall of their home so that they could provide a room for Elisha to stay in when he was in their area. Because of her generous spirit, God rewarded this woman who had no children by giving her a son. Several years later when the son died God rewarded her again by allowing Elisha to restore life to him. God will reward us for our willingness to share our home with others.

Heb. 13:1-2, "Let brotherly love continue. Be not forgetful to entertain strangers: for thereby some have entertained angels unawares." I believe that entertaining is a special gift God has given to me and our home has always been open to visitors, especially missionaries. I feel honored and blessed to have been able to share my home with these servants of God. I remember a Saturday afternoon many years ago when the Lord blessed me for opening my home to strangers. I had returned home from grocery shopping and I was trying to catch up on my wash and straighten up my house after having had company all week. Feeling exhausted and wondering how I could get everything done before Sunday, I knelt by my bed to pray. It was then that the phone rang and a missionary that I had never heard of asked directions to our church. Their family was passing through town and did not have a service the next day and wanted to visit our church. In our conversation he also asked if I knew of a reasonable motel where they might stay and immediately I invited them to come to our home.

When I hung up the phone I wondered if I was crazy. My house was not ready, the beds weren't even made, and I was so tired. How was I going to handle more company? The family soon knocked on my door and what a blessing they were to us that weekend. They did not care that my house was not spotless. They seemed to enjoy the simple meals I prepared and we had a great time of fellowship. On top of all that, the Lord answered my prayer and renewed my strength.

Remember when you entertain that everything does not have to be perfect. Keep things simple so that you won't become over-stressed. People feel more comfortable in normal, relaxed conditions than they do in some picture book setting. Just be yourself. Many women miss out on blessings because they fear their home is not good enough or that they will do something wrong. As a result they never open their home to guests and miss out on many blessings and friendships.

I Cor. 16:15, "I beseech you, brethren, (ye know the house of Stephanas, that it is the first fruits of Achaia, and that they have addicted themselves to the ministry of the saints.)" In this day of addictions wouldn't it be wonderful to have the addiction of ministering and giving. We have a dear friend who had little money yet she seemed to be addicted to giving money away. My husband used to tease her about looking for people with a need so that she could give them her grocery money. God blessed her for her giving and supplied her needs. Her three children never wore rags or went hungry and today none of them are addicted to drugs, alcohol or sex, but they have grown up to be generous Christians themselves. Her good example has paid off. What more could a mother ask. III John 4, "I have no greater joy than to hear that my children walk in truth." Be a good example to your children, your friends and acquaintances. Be a benevolent Christian lady.

Questions:

1. Because the Philippian church gave to Paul, the Lord promised in Phil. 4:19 to supply _____ their need.

2. The Macedonian church was able to give out of deep poverty because they "_____."

3. Prov. 11:25 says that "the liberal soul shall be made _____."

4. I John 3:17 tells us that to be unwilling to give means the _____ _____ does not dwell in us.

5. What woman gave her talent for sewing by making coats and garments for the widows? Acts. 9:36-39 _____

6. What does the Bible call the woman of Shunam because she fed and housed the prophet Elisha? II Kings 4:8-11 _____

7. Heb. 13:1-2 says we can show love by entertaining _____

8. The house of Stephanas had addicted themselves to the "_____ _____." I Cor. 16:15

Lesson Seven

"She is Discerning"

"She is Discerning"

"She openeth her mouth with wisdom." Proverbs 31:26

Webster's <u>1828 American Dictionary of the English Language</u> defines the word discern as "to see or understand the difference; to make distinction; as to discern between good and evil, truth and falsehood." The Proverbs 31 woman was certainly discerning in her speech. She knew what to say and when to say it. Not only did she speak wisely, she spoke kindly. Prov. 31:26, "She openeth her mouth with wisdom; and in her tongue is the law of kindness." As godly women we need this same kind of discernment today.

The Virtuous Woman Speaks in Wisdom

Her wisdom comes from within:
How can a woman open her mouth with wisdom? The book of Proverbs gives the answer to this question as it has much to say about being wise and speaking in wisdom. True wisdom comes from a heart that has been given to God and is controlled by the Holy Spirit. Prov. 2:6, "For the Lord giveth wisdom." Prov. 9:10, "The fear of the Lord is the beginning of wisdom." The words that come from the mouth of a person reveal what is in the heart of that person. Prov. 16:23, "The heart of the wise teaches his mouth, and addeth learning to his lips." Prov. 15:2, "The tongue of the wise useth knowledge aright: but the mouth of fools poureth out foolishness." Prov. 15:7, "The lips of the wise disperse knowledge: but the heart of the foolish doeth not so."

She thinks before she speaks:
Prov. 10:19, "...he that refrained his lips is wise." Prov. 29:11, "A fool uttered all his mind: but a wise man keepeth it in till afterwards." The woman who speaks before considering her words will later regret many things that she has said. The reality of the matter is that once words are spoken they can never be unspoken. Apologies can be made but the words cannot be erased. The discerning woman will think before she speaks.

She gains wisdom by listening:
Prov. 1:5, "A wise man will hear, and will increase learning." Prov. 12:15 "...he that hearkened unto counsel is wise." Prov. 13:1, "A wise son heareth his

father's instruction:" Prov. 13:10, "…with the well advised is wisdom." Prov. 15:31, "The ear that heareth the reproof of life abideth among the wise." Prov. 19:20, "Hear counsel, and receive instruction, that thou mayest be wise in thy latter end." Though we may sometimes think that we have all the answers there is much to be learned by listening to someone else's ideas and opinions. The discerning woman will be a good listener. She will consider the counsel of others and will not close her ear to correction.

She does not speak in anger:

Prov. 29:8, "…wise men turn away wrath." Prov. 15:1, "A soft answer turneth away wrath: but grievous words stir up anger." When we speak in anger we are prone to say hurtful words that should never be spoken. Words spoken in anger can cause others to sin because they are apt to answer with angry words. Once again, the damage that is done can never be undone. Eph. 4:26, "Be ye angry, and sin not:" The discerning woman will keep her mouth shut when she is angry.

She seeks wise friends:

Prov. 13:20, "He that walketh with wise men shall be wise." It is quite evident that friends do influence friends. If you spend time with people who gossip you will find it hard not to gossip. If you listen to bad language on a regular basis you may be surprised to hear those same words coming from your own mouth. Just as a chameleon lizard changes his colors to fit his surroundings we also have a tendency to take on the actions of those with whom we spend time. A discerning woman will choose wise friends who speak wise words which in turn help her to speak wise words. Of course, the wisest of all friends is God and we need to make Him our very best friend by spending much time fellowshipping with Him in prayer and Bible study. He is the friend that will never disappoint us. Prov. 18:24, "…there is a friend that sticketh closer than a brother." The closer we get to Him the more we will become like Him.

She is a blessing to others:

Prov. 12:18, "…but the tongue of the wise is health." The discerning woman who speaks words of wisdom will be a blessing to those around her. She will not be given to gossip, backbiting or criticism, but her words will be an encouragement to others and will help to heal the wounds of those who are suffering. As I Pet. 3:4 advises, she will adorn herself with "a meek and quiet spirit, which is in the sight of God of great price." This meek and quiet spirit is a mark of a discerning woman.

The Virtuous Woman Speaks in Kindness

She puts on kindness:

Prov. 31:26, "...in her tongue is the law of kindness." The discerning woman will make kindness a law in her life. She will determine to act and speak kindly. Col. 3:12 tells us to put on kindness and this indicates that a conscious effort must be made in order to be kind. We make that conscious effort by preparing our heart so that the Lord can fill our mouth with kind words. Prov. 16:1, "The preparations of the heart in man, and the answer of the tongue, is from the LORD."

Her love of God produces kindness:

I Cor. 13:4, "Charity (love) suffereth long (is patient), and is kind." God is the source of love and the woman who truly loves God will be enabled by God to love others and to speak in kindness. I John 5:2, "By this we know that we love the children of God, when we love God, and keep his commandments."

She forgives as an example of kindness:

Eph. 4:32, "And be ye kind one to another, tenderhearted, forgiving one another, even as God for Christ's sake hath forgiven you." God is the ultimate example of forgiveness. The godly woman will find strength in Him to be kind and forgive others.

She benefits from her kindness:

The old adage says "you can draw more flies with honey than you can with vinegar" and the same thing is true of kindness. The discerning woman who chooses to speak in kindness will greatly benefit from her choice. She will certainly have more friends and she will improve her health as well. A bitter spirit that produces harsh words can destroy one's health while love and kindness have the opposite affect. Prov. 16:24, "Pleasant (kind) words are as an honeycomb, sweet to the soul, and health to the bones."

Prov. 16:21, "The wise in heart shall be called prudent: and the sweetness of the lips increaseth learning."

Ps. 139:4, "For there is not a word in my tongue, but, lo, O LORD, thou knowest it altogether."

Questions:

1. According to Prov. 2:6, how do we get wisdom? _____

2. What is the beginning of wisdom? Prov. 9:10? _____

3. What does Prov. 29:11 tell us about a fool? _____
    _____

4. Prov. 12:15 tells us it is wise to _____.

5. To speak angry words is sin. Eph. 4:26 warns us to "Be ye angry, and
    _____.

6. It is important to choose _____
    friends. Prov. 13:20

7. Who is the wisest friend we can choose? _____

8. Prov. 12:18 says that "the tongue of the wise is _____."

9. The answer of our tongue should come from whom? _____."
    Prov. 16:1

10. Eph. 4:32 tells us to be _____ to one
    another and to _____ one another.

11. Prov. 16:24 says "Pleasant words are as an honeycomb, _____
    to the soul, and _____ to the bones."

Lesson Eight

"She is Praised"

"She is Praised"

"...let her own works praise her." Proverbs 31:31

The Virtuous Woman is Praised by Others

She is praised by her children:

Prov. 31:28, "Her children arise up, and call her blessed." On a tombstone in a little country cemetery in Florence, Mississippi, you will find this verse inscribed. This tombstone belongs to my mother-in-law, and this verse was selected by my husband, his brother and sister, because it described their feelings toward their Mother. She lived her life in such a way that her children could truly rise up and call her blessed.

Nowhere is a woman better known than in her own home where she lets down her hair and her true colors show. When her children, who know her for what she really is, call her blessed it is quite an accomplishment. I remember a letter that our oldest son, who was in the Navy at the time, wrote to my husband and me. In the letter he thanked us for being good parents and for providing him a stable home that he looked forward to visiting. Many of his comrades did not have this privilege because Dad lived one place and Mom lived somewhere else. I considered it the highest honor that I could receive to have our son praise us for the good example we had been to him.

In Eph. 6:1-2, the Bible teaches children to be obedient and respectful. "Children, obey your parents in the Lord: for this is right. Honour thy father and mother; which is the first commandment with promise." For a child to call his mother blessed is more than the dutiful respect commanded in this verse. It is an honor that every mother should strive to attain. The greatest task given to a mother is to be a godly example before her children. How sad that many mothers are never called blessed because they do not live a life that merit's the praise of their children.

She is praised by her husband:

Prov. 31:28b, "...her husband also, and he praiseth her." No one knows a woman better than her husband and to receive his praise means that she is doing something right. She should let him know that she cherishes his praise and should in turn praise him for the nice things he does for her.

She is praised for her good works:
Prov. 31:31, "Give her of the fruit of her hands; and let her own works praise her in the gates." We have already discussed the works of the Proverbs 31 woman. These consisted of her gardening, her sewing and her help given to the poor and needy. She was known and praised for her works in the gates of the city. The city gate was the place where the city's business was conducted. In a very small community it might be possible for a woman to be known at city hall for her good works, but since most of us live in larger communities, this could be a difficult goal to reach. It might be better to think of our local church, the place where our spiritual business is conducted, as the gate where we are praised for our good works. The godly woman should actively serve the Lord in her church. She should be willing to help out wherever she is needed.

Of course, good works have nothing to do with salvation. Eph. 2:8-9, "For by grace are ye saved through faith; and that not of yourselves; it is the gift of God: Not of works, lest any man should boast." Paul does, however, in Col. 1:10, when instructing the Christians at Colosse say, "That ye might walk worthy of the Lord unto all pleasing, being fruitful in every good work, and increasing in the knowledge of God."

She is praised for her virtue:
Prov. 31:29, "Many daughters have done virtuously, but thou excellest them all." In lesson one we defined virtue as being morally good and abstaining from vice. Even though the majority of people do not live moral lives today, and even though Christians are sometimes ridiculed for their moral standards; a morally pure woman will be respected and even praised for her virtuous life.

She is praised for her fear of the Lord:
Prov. 31:30, "Favour is deceitful, and beauty is vain: but a woman that feareth the LORD, she shall be praised." We live in a day when much emphasis is placed on outward beauty. Beautiful people often get special treatment that others do not receive. In God's sight, outward beauty is deceitful and vain. It is the woman that

fears God that will receive the praise of God. This does not mean that a woman should neglect her outward appearance, but much more time should be spent making herself pleasing to God than is spent making herself pleasing in the sight of man.

When a woman fears the Lord she will have so much respect for the Lord that she will trust Him in every aspect of her life. I Pet. 3:5 says that the holy women of old trusted God enough to be in subjection to their own husbands. If the fear of the Lord helped the women of old, can it not help us to do the same today? Prov. 14:26 says, "In the fear of the LORD is strong confidence." This is not self-confidence, but rather confidence in the Lord.

The Virtuous Woman Does Not Praise Herself

Prov. 27:2, "Let another man praise thee, and not thine own mouth: a stranger and not thine own lips." The godly woman will be content with the praise others offer her and will not praise herself by boasting about her accomplishments.

Boasting is a sign of pride:
According to Prov. 6:16-17, pride is one of the things that God hates. Prov. 16:18 says, "Pride goeth before destruction and a haughty spirit before a fall." Prov. 14:3, "In the mouth of the foolish is a rod of pride.

Boasting is foolish:
Prov. 30:32, "If thou hast done foolishly in lifting up thyself, or if thou hast thought evil, lay thine hand upon thy mouth." The discerning woman who thinks before she speaks will not be likely to boast. In II Cor. 11:16-17 Paul says, "I say again, Let no man think me a fool; if otherwise, yet as a fool receive me, that I may boast myself a little. That which I speak, I speak it not after the Lord, but as it were foolishly, in this confidence of boasting."

Boasting is trusting in self:
Boasting is taking self-credit for that which rightfully belongs to God. We may be able to accomplish a lot of things in the flesh but without God giving us life, health, intellect, talent and ability where would we be? With all of the resources and

abilities that we might have, we do not have the ability to redeem our soul. Ps. 49:6-8, "They that trust in their wealth, and boast themselves in the multitude of their riches; None of them can by any means redeem his brother, nor give to God a ransom for him: (For the redemption of their soul is precious, and it ceaseth for ever:)"

Boasting is evil:

Jam. 4:16, "But now ye rejoice in your boastings: all such rejoicing is evil." The godly woman will ask God's help in the matter of boasting that she might not praise herself, but that she might instead glory in Christ. I Cor. 1:31, "He that glorieth, let him glory in the Lord." Gal. 6:14, "But God forbid that I should glory, save in the cross of our Lord Jesus Christ, by who the world is crucified unto me, and I unto the world."

I trust that this study of the virtuous woman of Proverbs 31 will motivate you to be a virtuous woman yourself. There are many other godly women in the Bible that we can learn from and it would be good to study their lives as well. Here are a few that you might consider:

- Hannah: The Woman Who Prayed, I Sam. 1-2
- Sarah: The Woman of Faith, Heb. 11:11, Gen. 21:22
- Deborah: The Woman Who Judged, Jud. 4-5
- Esther: The Woman Who Saved a Nation, Esther
- Dorcas: The Woman Who Gave, Acts 9:36-41
- Martha: The Woman Who Served, Luke 10:38-42, John 12:2
- Mary of Bethany: The Woman Who Worshipped, Luke 10:39, John 12:3-8

None of these women were perfect but because they gave their lives to the Lord He found them worthy of mention in the Bible. The encouraging message for us is, that in spite of our imperfections, God can use us today if we will yield to His Lordship.

Questions:

1. The virtuous woman's children will call her _____.
   Prov. 31:28

2. Eph. 6:1-2 commands children to _____ and _____
   their parents.

3. For what was the virtuous woman praised in the gates? _____
   Prov. 31:31

4. Prov. 31:30 says that "_____ is deceitful, and
   beauty is _____."

5. "A woman that _____, she shall
   be praised.

6. Prov. 14:26 says, "In the fear of the Lord is _____."

7. Prov. 27:2, says to let _____ give you
   praise and not _____.

8. Prov. 30:32 says that it is _____ to lift
   up yourself.

9. To rejoice in your boastings is _____.
   Jam. 4:16

10. Our glorying should be in _____.
    I Cor. 1:31

Made in the USA
Lexington, KY
27 February 2017